Winchester, in the heart of Hampshire, is England's ancient capital.
Home to just 40,000 inhabitants, I have lived here for over ten years.
I was married here, my children were born here and my business
began here.

I feel I owe something to this beautiful city, and so this is my
illustrated tribute to the historical, captivating, wonderful Winchester.

All illustrations are available as prints.
www.simonharmer.co.uk

For Jess, Charlie & Wellington

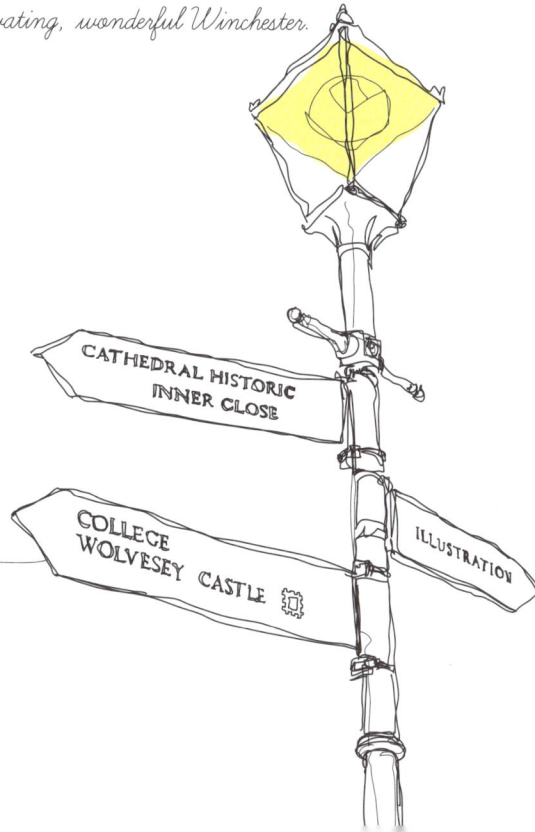

CATHEDRAL HISTORIC
INNER CLOSE

COLLEGE
WOLVESEY CASTLE

ILLUSTRATION

ÆLFRED

King Alfred

I see this wonderfully imposing bronze statue of Winchester's famous
King every day. Designed by Hamo Thornycroft, it has stood proud over
the Broadway since 1901. Alfred the Great was King of Wessex from 871
to 899, during which time he led his armies against numerous Viking raids.

He is fondly remembered not only for his brave military endeavours,
but also for his social, educational and legal reforms.

He is, of course, more famously known for burning cakes!

The Guildhall

The Guildhall soars high above The Broadway, with its now green, copper covered clock tower. The construction of this audaciously Gothic building began in 1871 and was opened by Lord Selborne, in May 1873.

The site belongs to the City Council, and is a regular venue for large and small functions, from weddings to beer festivals!

The City Mill

Sitting on the River Itchen, this restored mill has roots tracing back to the Domesday Book in 1086. The mill was in use up until the early 20th century, having been rebuilt in 1744.

Now owned by the National Trust, the mill underwent a significant restoration programme, which concluded in 2004. This meant that after 90 years, the mill was finally milling flour again.

As well as seeing the mill in action, visitors might also be lucky enough to see the local otters, who frequent the mill and surrounding river banks.

Wolvesey Castle

This delightfully ruinous landmark is surprisingly well hidden in Winchester - tucked discretely away behind the cathedral, and accessed via a small path on College Street. Wolvesey Castle was erected by the Bishop of Winchester, Henry of Blois between 1130 and 1140. It was understood to have been destroyed by Roundheads during the English Civil War in 1646. The castle is currently owned by English Heritage.

Be warned, there are no drawbridges or dungeons - there isn't even a moat! That said, it is still an impressive place to visit, and a reminder of Winchester's glorious history.

Winchester College

Winchester College, the independent boarding school, is one of the oldest schools in England, with over 600 years of history.

It is one of the original nine English public schools defined by the Public Schools Act 1868. The school holds a real air of mystery, with its walled gardens and stately gates.

Founded by William of Wykeham, Bishop of Winchester in 1382, it now has 10 boarding houses, each with its own nickname, including Kenny's, Cook's, and Hopper's

St Cross Hospital

Nestled in the beautifully tranquil setting of the water meadows, the Hospital of St Cross is considered the oldest charitable institution in the United Kingdom, and the largest medieval almshouse in the country. Originally founded around 1132, for `thirteen poor men, feeble and so reduced in strength that they can scarcely or not at all support themselves without other aid´.

The Grade I listed buildings are now open to the public, and the thirteen Brothers still reside in the Brethren´s lodgings.

Kingsgate

Kingsgate and Westgate are the two surviving medieval gates in Winchester, the former having its name first recorded in 1148, and taking its name from being the entrance to the royal palace.

The current gate is thought to date from the 14th century. It sits underneath the small church of St Swithun-upon-Kingsgate, which was built in the Middle Ages.

Winchester Cathedral

This spectacular cathedral is possibly Winchester's most iconic landmark. The Cathedral Church of the Holy Trinity, St Peter, St Paul and St Swithun (to give it its full name) dates from 1079, and is the seat of the Bishop of Winchester and the Mother Church of the Diocese.

The cathedral boasts Europe's longest nave, and is the burial place of many of England's historical figures, including King Canute and Jane Austen. On a lighter note, the beautifully ethereal Antony Gormley sculpture, Sound II is housed in the cathedral crypt which occasionally floods, creating an even more surreal atmosphere.

The cathedral was effectively saved from collapsing in 1906 by an extraordinary man, William Walker. A deep sea diver by trade, William spent six years diving underneath the cathedral to lay concrete bags, so that the walls could be underpinned and prevented from sinking into the watery peat foundations.

The Buttercross

Also known as The High Cross or City Cross, this 15th Century cross was once used as a site to sell produce, hence the name Buttercross. In 1770 it was sold off by the Paving Commissioners to a Mr Dummer. When he tried to remove it, the citizens of Winchester organised a small riot and preserved the monument for the City.

Restored in 1865, and now a Scheduled Ancient Monument, legend has it that if you sit on the Buttercross you will never leave Winchester.

The Westgate

The original city plan, devised by Alfred the Great, contained four main city gates, in the north, east, south and west. The Westgate is the only gate left standing today. It was rebuilt in the 12th century and modified later. From the 16th to the 18th century its main use was as a local prison, and graffiti engraved on its stone walls can still be seen from this period.

The Westgate is now a museum, containing many interesting artefacts and boasting glorious views down the High Street towards Alfred himself.

The Great Hall

The stunning medieval Great Hall was originally part of Winchester Castle, and was built by Henry III in the 13th century. The Castle itself was damaged by fire in 1302, and, following the Civil War, Oliver Cromwell ordered that the defences of the Castle be dismantled. Charles II later demolished the remaining structure so that he could build his palace on the site, but left the Great Hall in place.

The roof was replaced in 1873, and the Hall now contains the Round Table and a statue of Queen Victoria by Albert Gilbert, dating from 1887. A re-creation of a medieval herber (Queen Eleanor's garden) is now located at the rear of the Hall.